The Piano Player

Uplifting Classics

20 of the most famous pieces of classical music to lift the spirits, specially arranged for intermediate piano solo

Contents

04 I Vow to Thee, My Country – Gustav Holst

05 The Blue Danube Waltz (Op. 314) – Johann Strauss II

08 Sheep May Safely Graze (from the *Hunting Cantata*) (BWV 208) – Johann Sebastian Bach

10 Ride of the Valkyries (from *Die Walküre*) (WWV 86B) – Richard Wagner

12 Wedding March (from *A Midsummer Night's Dream*) (Op. 61) – Felix Mendelssohn

13 Triumphal March (from *Aida*) – Giuseppe Verdi

14 Hungarian Dance No. 5 in F♯ minor – Johannes Brahms

16 Ode to Joy (from *Symphony No. 9*) – Ludwig van Beethoven

18 William Tell Overture – Gioachino Rossini

19 Scherzo (from *Piano Sonata in G minor*) – Clara Schumann

24 Mazurka in C major (Op. 33, No. 3) – Frédéric Chopin

26 Nimrod (from *Enigma Variations*) (Op. 36) – Edward Elgar

28 Zadok the Priest (Coronation Anthem No.1) (HWV 258) – George Frideric Handel

31 Can-Can (from *Orpheus in the Underworld*) – Jacques Offenbach

36 Radetzky March (Op. 228) – Johann Strauss I

40 Rondo Alla Turca (from *Sonata No.11 in A major*) (K. 331) – Wolfgang Amadeus Mozart

46 The Liberty Bell March – John Philip Sousa

51 In the Hall of the Mountain King (Suite No. 1 from *Peer Gynt*) (Op. 46: IV) – Edvard Grieg

56 Les Toréadors (Suite No. 1 from *Carmen*) – Georges Bizet

60 The Arrival of the Queen of Sheba (from *Solomon*) (HWV 67) – George Frideric Handel

© 2023 by Faber Music Ltd
This edition first published by Faber Music Ltd in 2023
Brownlow Yard
12 Roger Street
London WC1N 2JU
Cover artwork: *The Peacock and the Magpie* (from 'Aesop's Fables' series)
© Estate of Edward Bawden.
Supplied by Trustees of the Cecil Higgins Art Gallery (The Higgins Bedford)
Cover design by Adam Hay Studio
Portrait of Edward Bawden by Brenda Herdman
Credit: Fry Art Gallery, Saffron Walden, Essex, UK.
© Fry Art Gallery Society / Bridgeman Images
Printed in England by Caligraving Ltd
All rights reserved

ISBN10: 0-571-54201-8
EAN13: 978-0-571-54201-7

To buy Faber Music publications or to find out about the full range of titles available
please contact your local music retailer or Faber Music sales enquiries:

Faber Music Ltd, Burnt Mill, Elizabeth Way, Harlow CM20 2HX
Tel: +44 (0) 1279 82 89 82
fabermusic.com

Edward Bawden
CBE RA (1903–1989)

Edward Bawden was one of the foremost British artists and designers of the mid twentieth century. His work ranged widely across a variety of media, and he believed there was no real distinction between the fine and the commercial arts.

Bawden attended the Cambridge School of Art (1918–22) and the Royal College of Art School of Design (1922–26), where he was a contemporary of Eric Ravilious and a student of Paul Nash. He worked throughout his life as a painter and printmaker, with commissions for murals, posters, wallpaper, book illustration and graphic design; most notably for London Transport, Shell, Fortnum & Mason and the Curwen Press.

His sense of design, as well as a mischievous wit, are apparent in the imaginative patterns and bold lines of his linocuts and drawings; his watercolours are made up of shapes and patterns of colour and light.

During the Second World War, Bawden served as an Official War Artist. He was in France with the British Army until the evacuation of Dunkirk and after that in North Africa and the Middle East. Previously reluctant to draw people, he was now forced to acquire these skills and produced portraits and figurative scenes in watercolour.

Bawden lived in Great Bardfield, Essex from the 1930s to 1970. While there, he was an important member of the Great Bardfield Artists. He then moved to Saffron Walden where he continued to work until the end of his life.

Both The Fry Art Gallery in Saffron Walden and The Higgins in Bedford hold a substantial collection of Bawden's work, which is also represented in numerous public and private collections, including the Imperial War Museum, the Tate, and the Victoria & Albert Museum.

We are delighted that The Estate of Edward Bawden, along with The Higgins Art Gallery & Museum Bedford, have allowed Faber Music to feature a selection of Bawden's striking works on the covers of The Piano Player series.

I Vow to Thee, My Country

Composed by Gustav Holst

The Blue Danube Waltz (Op. 314)

Composed by Johann Strauss II

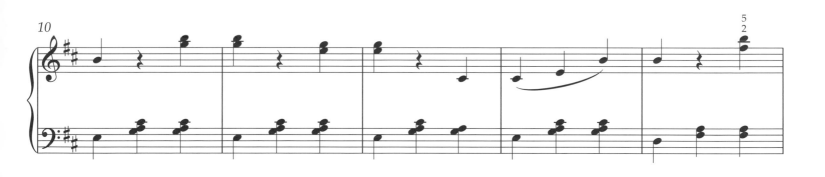

D.C. al Fine

Sheep May Safely Graze

(from the *Hunting Cantata*) (BWV 208)

Composed by Johann Sebastian Bach

Ride of the Valkyries

(from *Die Walküre: Der Ring des Nibelungen*) (WWV 86B)

Composed by Richard Wagner

Wedding March

(from *A Midsummer Night's Dream*) (Op. 61)

Composed by Felix Mendelssohn

Triumphal March

(from *Aida*)

Composed by Giuseppe Verdi

Hungarian Dance No. 5 in F♯ minor

Composed by Johannes Brahms

Ode to Joy

(from *Symphony No. 9*)

Composed by Ludwig van Beethoven

William Tell Overture

Composed by Gioachino Rossini

Scherzo

(from *Piano Sonata in G minor*)

Composed by Clara Schumann

Mazurka in C major (Op. 33, No. 3)

Composed by Frédéric Chopin

Nimrod

(from *Enigma Variations*) (Op. 36)

Composed by Edward Elgar

Zadok the Priest

(Coronation Anthem No.1) (HWV 258)

Composed by George Frideric Handel

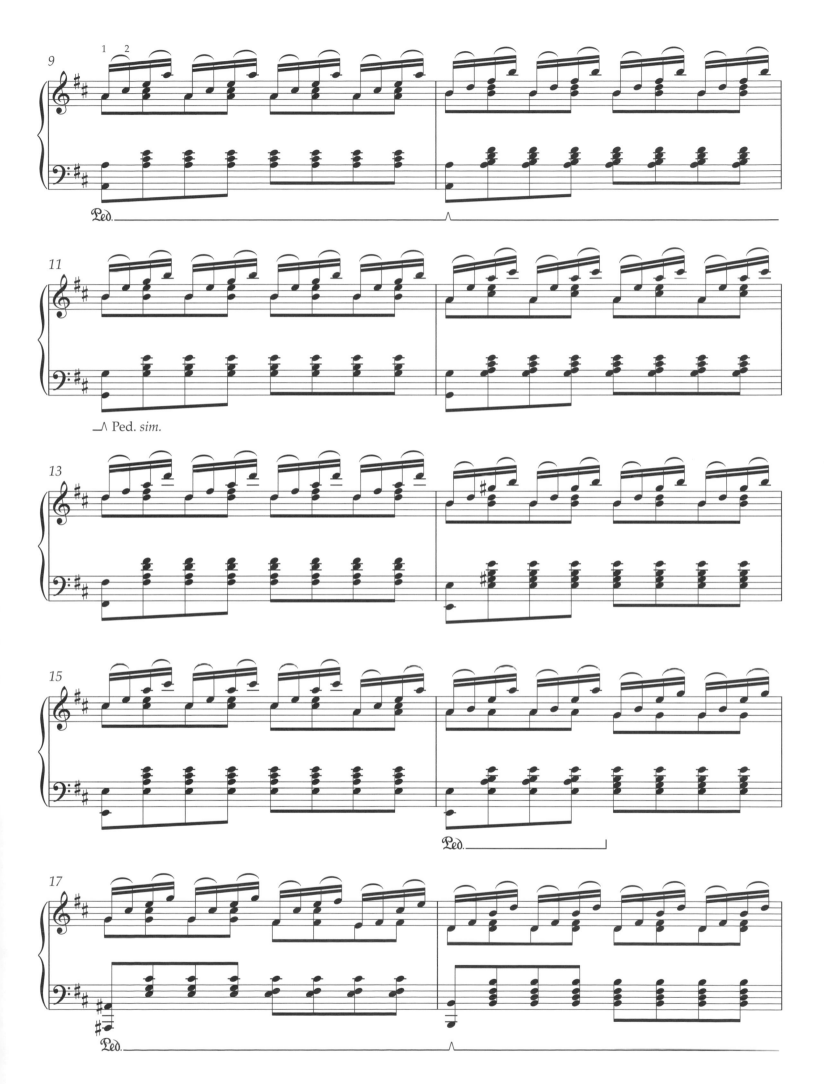

Can-Can

(from *Orpheus in the Underworld*)

Composed by Jacques Offenbach

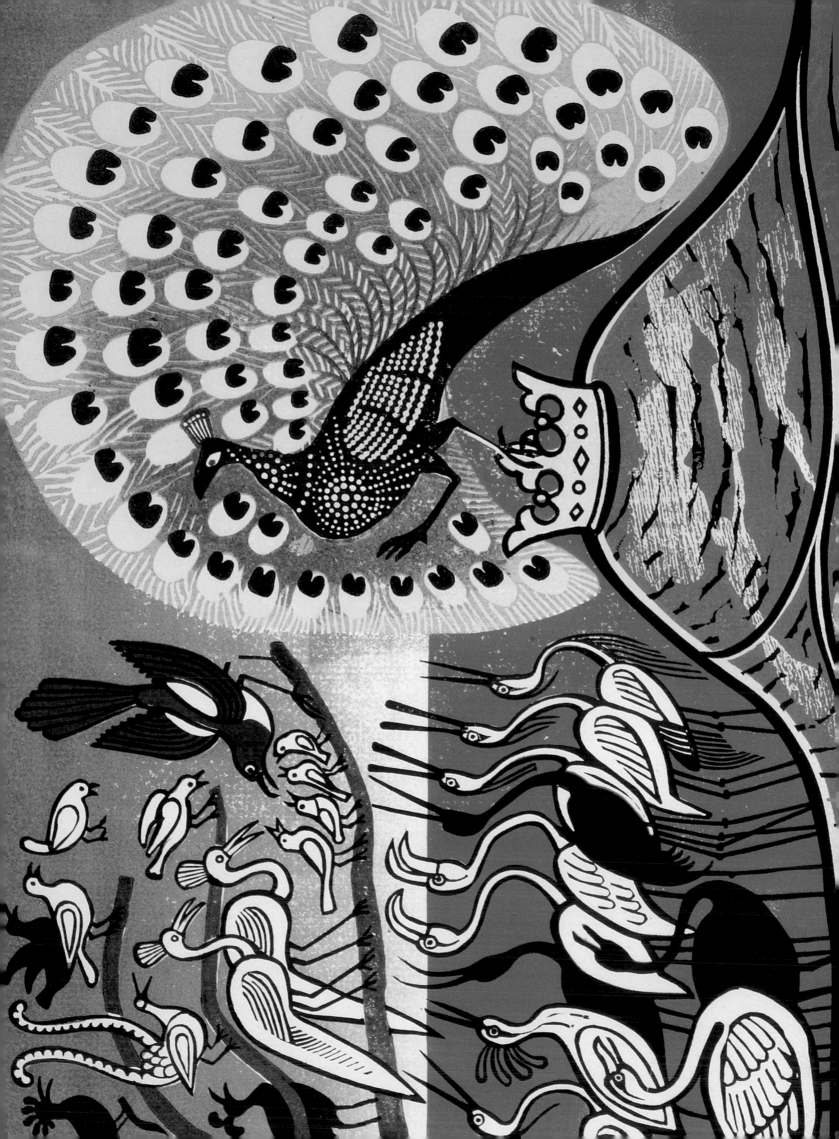

The Piano Player series

Seven wonderful collections of some of the greatest classical music
ever written, specially arranged for the intermediate pianist.
Each with its own collectible pull-out print of the
striking Edward Bawden cover artwork.

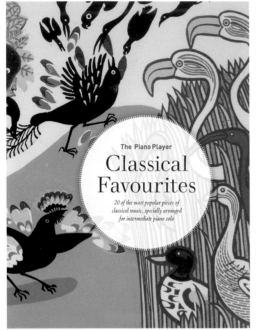

Classical Favourites
0-571-54200-X

British Classics
0-571-54169-0

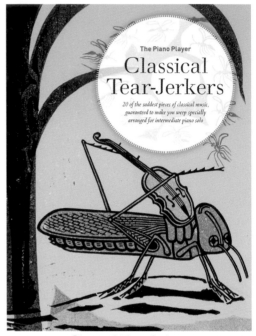

Classical Tear-Jerkers
0-571-54202-6

Classical Chillout
0-571-54203-4

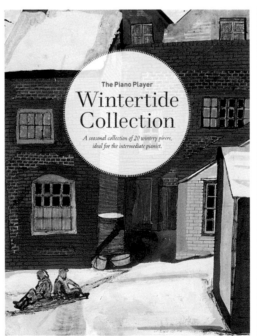

Wintertide Collection
0-571-54204-2

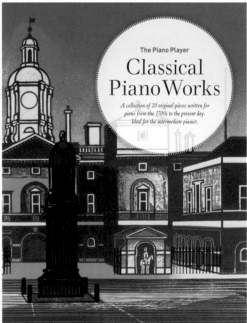

Classical Piano Works
0-571-54205-0

FABER **ff** MUSIC

Buy *The Piano Player* series online and from all good retailers.
Search 'Faber Music Piano Player' or visit fabermusic.com

The Peacock and the Magpie (from 'Aesop's Fables' series)

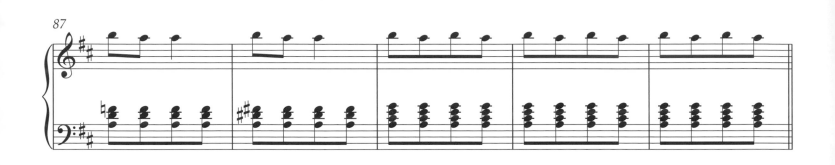

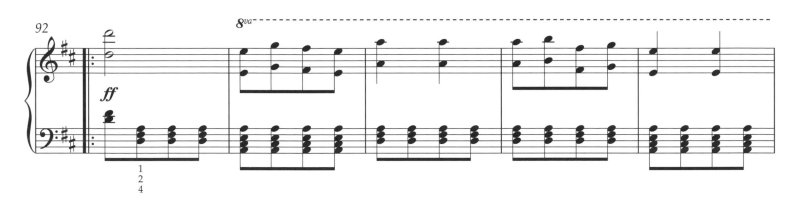

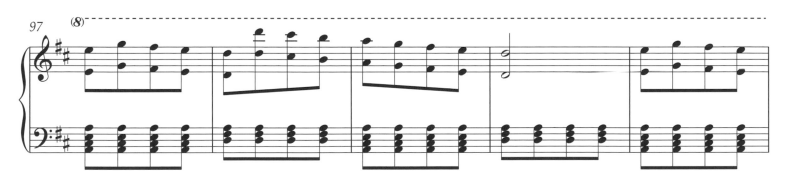

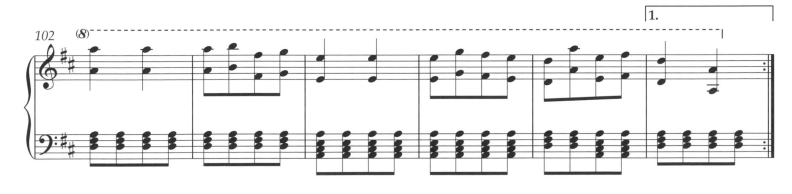

Radetzky March (Op. 228)

Composed by Johann Strauss I

Allegro ♩ = 109

Rondo Alla Turca

(from *Sonata No.11 in A major*) (K. 331)

Composed by Wolfgang Amadeus Mozart

The Liberty Bell March

Composed by John Philip Sousa

In the Hall of the Mountain King

(Suite No. 1 from *Peer Gynt*) (Op. 46: IV)

Composed by Edvard Grieg

Alla marcia e molto marcato ♩ = 138

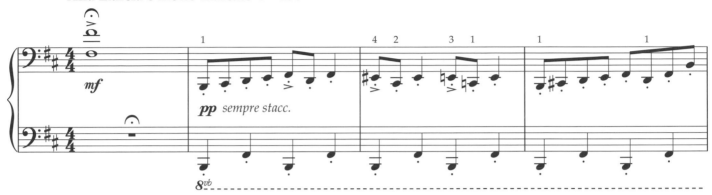

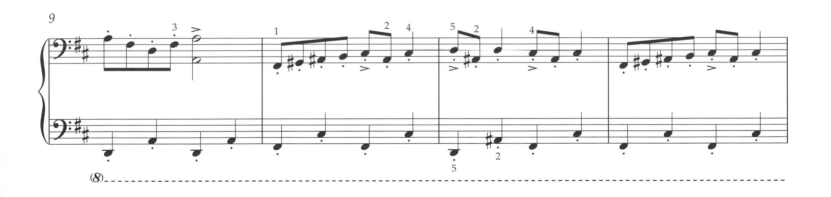

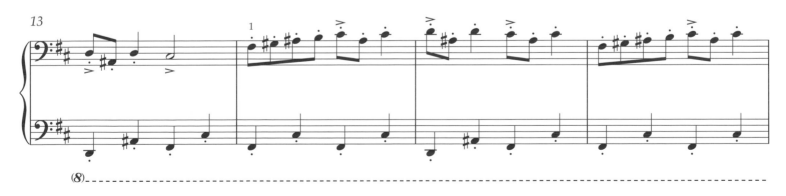

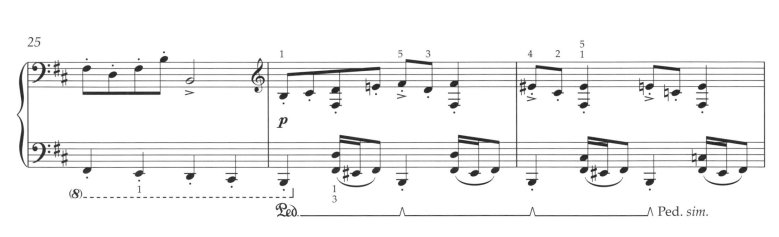

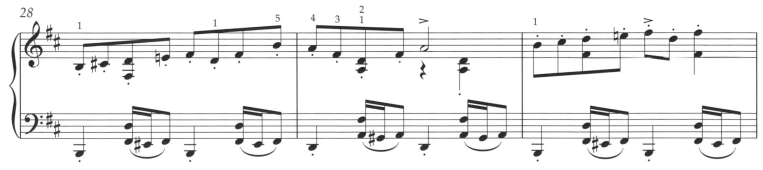

Les Toréadors

(Suite No. 1 from *Carmen*)

Composed by Georges Bizet

The Arrival of the Queen of Sheba

(from *Solomon*) (HWV 67)

Composed by George Frideric Handel

col 8va bassa ad lib -

Fine